SLEEPWALK™
LIVE IN THE DREAM

A 9-step Program of Self Destruction

SLEEPWALK™ — Live in the Dream
A 9-step Program of Self Destruction
Copyright © 2021 Stephen Renwick.

Renwick Fitness
Hub 13 A, Pepper House,
Pepper Road, Hazel Grove,
Stockport, SK7 5DP
www.renwick.fitness

Printed by Amazon KDP
ISBN: 9798498693910
Independently Published
First printing, 2021.

Book Design: Charlotte Mouncey www.bookstyle.co.uk

Thanks to:

Steve French for the creative support

Alan Partridge for 20 years of laughter.

SLEEPWALK™
LIVE IN THE DREAM

A 9-step Program of Self Destruction

STEPHEN RENWICK

DISCLAIMER:

This book is based on actual life events and is written as a parody of self-help guides. Please do not take the advice literally. However, if you want to avoid screwing up your life, I have much experience to share. My focus is to make this at least entertaining, as dark humour got me through dark times.

Contents

SUE'S SON SAYS:

If you are secure at all points,
you are lying to yourself.
If you have superior strength,
remind yourself you lack where it counts.
If you are temperamental,
that's good.
Pretend to be weak,
so that girls think you are sensitive.
If you are taking your ease,
take more eases.
If your forces are united,
tell them you don't like their wives.
If sovereign and subject are in accord,
get angry at those who care.
Attack yourself where you are loved,
appear where you are not welcome.

~ Sue's Son; *The Art of Self Destruction*

Introduction

A LOT OF US THINK we have made mistakes in our lives. Some of us might fancy ourselves as a bit of a f*ck-up. Or we might look at specific chapters in our life and say, *yep, f*cked that one up.*

We all have the incredible potential to let ourselves and others down. Most of us have tasted the bittersweet allure of, *I know I can do better, but do I want to?*

But how many of us play the game professionally? How many of us can achieve such a level of "f*ck-up" notoriety that kids want to wear our t-shirt and say our name, and when girls see us, they say, "Oh my god, that guy is a *complete* f*ck-up"?

This degree of "up" to which one must f*ck, is attainable only by a rare few. It's an elite club. And like any club, to become a member, you must prove your (lack of self-) worth before you can even apply.

In this book, we will walk you through the steps of f*cking up on a monumental scale and frequency. By the end of it, if you follow the steps correctly, even *you* will shake your head and ask yourself, "How could I have let this happen?"

I have no interest in the guy who ruins his marriage but otherwise does OK. I bow to the "broad-sweeper", he who destroys his friendships, reputation, bank account, credit, and his marriage, all in the same year. That's my kind of guy.

You can be that guy. *Anyone* can be.

And let's be fair to the ladies. Hollow, shallow, empty wins are not gender-specific.

Some of these wins — and, yeah, let's reframe the word here and deny society the tools it uses to judge us — will be small, and some will be major. They all have value. The trick is to diversify. Every win counts — big or small. They all withdraw from the same account.

In this book, we will review and analyse: the "botch", the "screw-up", the "f*ck-up", the "cluster-f*ck", and, of course, the "royal f*ck-up". You will learn various techniques to achieve each one. You will become familiar with how each one erodes your well-being and self-esteem. And these will eventually force a personal reckoning probably too late in life to do much about.

It took me 20 years and cost me — I have no earthly idea how much — to amass this information. I'm going to share my wisdom with you here so that, on my deathbed, I can look back and say, "Ah, yeah, maybe I shouldn't have done that."

If you want to f*ck up your life. If you want to spoil all that was ever good. If you want to precisely know the wrong things to do to squander the joys of health, finance, life balance, friendships, love, and happiness — all the trappings weaker people cling to — this book is for you.

All you must do is follow my patented and proven 9-step program for throwing it all away: SLEEPWALK™.

Spend. Leave. Engines. Education. Plates. Wagers. Awaken. Look inward. KFC.

When we SLEEPWALK™, we are in a permanent state of delusion. We think life is beautiful and bountiful, and we advance confidently through our existence in ignorant bliss. Yet the truth is we are asleep at the wheel. We don't see where we really are or where we are headed. We are oblivious to the perils of blindly living the dream and the hurt we cause as we careen through everything and everyone we ever held dear.

SLEEPWALK™ your way to hollow victories.

SLEEPWALK™ your way to empty trophies.

SLEEPWALK™ your way to shallow relationships.

Read this book. Drink it in. Eat it if you must. Absorb its wisdom. It's your life; you can ruin it however you like — and take as much time as you like doing it. But if you want a full dose of emptiness — an express ticket to nowhere — listen to me. If I can f*ck up *so* badly *so* quickly, *anyone* can. Trust me.

I believe in you. You can do this. This is your chance.

Don't f*ck this up.

Step 1 — SPEND

SPEND IS THE FIRST STEP in the program because, no matter who we are or what we earn, every one of us can spend more than we bring in. This is a step we can all practice, even if we are entirely new to self-destruction.

This deficit-forward practice is not only critical to our goal of financial ruin, but it also serves as a metaphor for future steps. On every level, we will need to create a balance sheet and ensure that every transaction degrades us in one way or another.

More on that later. For now, let's focus on f*cking up our finances.

CHOICES

We live in a world of garish capitalism, relentless marketing, sex and glamour in the mainstream media, and enviable lifestyles on social media. When we compare our everyday, humdrum existence to the polished world spoon-fed to us through our iPhones, we don't look great.

So, we must choose.

We can either embrace the visceral reaction we have to the images we see online and conclude that *we* are the failure for not having ALL those things right now.

Or we can take a moment to rationalise: These images, ad campaigns, movies, Instagram moments, and other desperate attempts by others to gain attention are created by thousands of people, possibly spending millions on developing. them And they are broadcast to an over-saturated media-scape that our primitive lizard brains are simply not evolved enough to compartmentalise.

Most likely, we blame ourselves.

Society's pressure does that to us. And we don't like that feeling. So, we seek ways to address the problem and soothe the pain. And like a junkie in need of a fix, or a kid seeking a sugar-high, we SPEND — because new things immediately feel good. Purchases are emotional band-aids when we feel like a failure. We buy cars, jewellery, Rolex watches, and multiple giant T.V. screens to join the club we see in the media and appear successful in this game called life.

Of course, the sugar-high — the fix — is short-lived. We all know that. So, soon, we are faced with another choice: move on from thinking that consuming retail goods is a sustainable solution or spend more.

If we want to f*ck up our life, we must SPEND.

We must write it on a post-it and stick it to our mirror.

Designer clothes, watches, nice cars (that require lots of premium fuel) are all opportunities to deplete capital. And then we can double down: these things require insurance, safekeeping, and upkeep.

Furthermore, the pseudo-lifestyle we are now starting to project feeds our persona of success and inflates our ego and stress levels. At the same time, thanks to the partnership of finance companies, it ramps up our debt.

DEBT

Depressed Egos on Borrowed Time.

The key is to build up debt and loans, reduce our ability to save money, and allow our subconscious to accept an artificially inflated sense of self as the new normal. D.E.B.T. is essential for our journey to oblivion.

Do you know what Big Debt sounds like? We want people to talk about the size of our debt.

Renting in a high-demand location is another excellent avenue to explore and has multiple benefits. There is the high rent, of course. Then there are the retail stores that circle like vultures. And if Gucci and Vivienne Westwood are just a car service away, so much the better. If we do this for a decade, we are well on our way to bankruptcy.

Try to buy stuff that has no intrinsic value.
If we buy a Rolex, it maintains its value. Not good.
On the other hand, meals, diamonds, first-class
travel tickets, designer clothes, and gifts have little
or no resale value. These purchases limit the risk of
amassing assets we can sell later
when we need cash.

TASTE

Later in this book, I'll dedicate an entire chapter to food. But fine dining — not part of that step — is an element of SPEND that deserves a paragraph here.

A fantastic way to burn through revenue is to develop expensive taste. There isn't a more refined way to do that than with fine dining — an asset in our portfolio of self-sabotage. High-end dining not only provides an opportunity to spend without resale options, but it also has the insidious effects of pandering to our ego and projecting fake success to our friends and family.

What more intoxicating request is there than "Would Sir like another bottle of the Richenbourg '49... excellent choice, I might add."

These "friendship treats" provide spectacular contributions to the monthly deficit. And whenever the spending feels a little stressful, use the credit card.

The use of credit cards helps repress the realisation that we are spending our own money. Plus, we can increase the spending limit when ready to up our debt game.

MINDSET

Everything we have discussed so far fits into the "screw-up" category. No single suggestion in this chapter is financially devastating. It's the attitude — the lifestyle — that can, and *must*, be adopted if we are to screw up seriously. Each purchase is like a hammer and chisel in the hands of a sculptor tap-tap-tapping away at his masterpiece.

And what is that masterpiece? The bottomless pit of low self-esteem and deep unhappiness that comes from leading a life that lacks any semblance of authenticity.

The first step on our way to f*cking up our life is to nurture an ironclad belief that money will make us happy. We must prioritise our desire to impress others with that money.

IN CLOSING

I did this for many years in the pursuit of happiness and acceptance. These material possessions yielded neither. This reality is essential to embrace as we embark on our journey to feeling empty.

STEP 2 — LEAVE

IN SPEND, WE TALKED ABOUT creating a vehicle for destruction. In LEAVE, we unbuckle our seat belt.

If we want to f*ck up our lives, we can employ many techniques and strategies to advance our cause. However, we cannot drown if we cling to a life raft or have someone cling to us. Put another way: for whom do you have more respect, the tightrope walker or the tightrope walker with no safety net?

This chapter will expose the perils of emotional bonds, loyalty, love, and friendship. We will examine how relationships can sabotage our downward mobility. And we will arm ourselves with techniques to eliminate emotional support.

Friends can intervene, talk to us, and dissuade us. They can provide "perspective" and balance. Though well-intended, we may not wish to be saved or forced to listen to their concerns. Worst of all, they have the power and organisational resources to hold interventions. These actions are the enemy of self-destructive desire and require swift and effective management.

The trick to ensuring against such unwanted interference is to sever the relationships. Emotionally we must LEAVE. We must f*ck up our friendships.

HOME TRUTHS

Since we were children, we have been indoctrinated in the "benefits" of sharing, manners, conscience, and loving support "networks". If we want to f*ck up our lives, we must ensure the "net" does *not* work. We want destruction, not distraction, and definitely not affection. Nor do we want the burden of breaking these bonds ourselves, leaving others "worried" and open to talk.

We need ways to guarantee the breaks are unfixable. We need to get personal.

H O T   T I P

Speak painful home truths. Tell stories that will cut to the bone. These will force the hand of our soon-to-be former friends through passive aggression. Make THEM leave. Reverse the psychology.

To develop savage skills in savaging relationships, we must go beyond passively avoiding drinking from the well of love; we must actively poison it for others. Home truths draw blood with minimal effort. I recommend memorising the U.T.I. method.

U.T.I.: upset friends — tell secrets — insult significant others.

Typically, U.T.I.s will erode, if not completely erase, any obligation others feel towards us.[1] Our friends will do the heavy

---

1   More accurately, U.T.I.s sting the victim and introduce a fear of interaction.

lifting and avoid further interaction. And we will be on the road to isolation, depression, and hopelessness.

And while we are here, let's discuss strategic thinking that can reduce our workload and increase efficacy. If we are wise, we can kill two friendships (or three, or ten) with one stone-cold home truth.

H O T   T I P

> When we prioritise key targets that can influence others, we instigate a "mass leaving event" that can send shudders through our social and family circles for years.

Breaking through social niceties and poking at real feelings are techniques that will, with practice, become second nature and devastatingly devastating.

Allow me to be specific: I once applied a textbook U.T.I. assassination of a best friend of thirty-five years by targeting his new wife. The primary goal of severing the most important friendship in my life was strong work. The secondary and tertiary waves of goodbyes from upset family and friends were profound and long-lasting achievements.

JEALOUSY

Fomenting jealousy is another hammer in our toolkit. Its strength lies in how unnecessary it is. For this, I recommend we familiarise ourselves with the M.R.I. technique.

Manifest Righteous Indignation.

For example:

Step 1: Refuse to acknowledge the good fortunes of others, such as an acquisition of a status symbol like a sports car. This dismissal establishes tension.

Step 2: Next, visit with our own new status symbol that outshines theirs. This releases tension in the form of righteous indignation.

Step 3: Brag. Rub proverbial salt in their wounded ego: tension.

Step 4: LEAVE. This will leave your loved one with no other option: to release through social and family discourse.

Tension and release. Tension and release.

HOT TIP

Continue to post, promote, and advertise your status symbol on the enemy's social media for a prolonged campaign to encourage a potential mass leaving event.

Just like many other steps in my SLEEPWALK™ 9-step program, diversification is the secret to full-coverage, Agent Orange-style weed whacking. While there may be a silver bullet technique for f*cking up our life, the professional does not assume so. Nor does he wait around for one — the professional presses on, pushing at every stress point.

COVERT OPS

A respite from some of the harsher methods discussed above can be relaxing. Yet these times are even sweeter with honey, especially someone else's ex-honey. Befriending the ex-friend of a friend or family member can be as bitter for them as it is sweet for us.

Back-stabbing is perhaps the only good reason for making new "low-level" friends: to hurt higher-level ones. Posting selfies from their home has an insidious, gnawing effect on others.

HOT TIP

Promoting paranoia and jealousy in others can expedite LEAVING EVENTS. Leaving group chats is a great irritant, as is acting as if nothing happened.

IN CLOSING

When taken in combination, LEAVE is a mighty cocktail that yields a cruel hangover. If we want to f*ck up our life and can master only one step, LEAVE is the one to master. There's nothing better than experiencing life alone.

I did it all.

It's why I'm the author of this book, and you are the reader.

STEP 3 — ENGINES

STRICTLY SPEAKING, ENGINES COULD BE a paragraph in SPEND. However, the pure sex of sports cars, and the multi-layered opportunities these cluster-f*cks offer, make them deserving of their own chapter.

Freud talks about the "tip of the iceberg" — the bit people see. More than anything else, our ENGINE is the key metric other people use to gauge our success. Know that. Learn that. Use that.

In ENGINES, we will cover some of the various ways ENGINES can hasten our financial crash and impress our friends at the same time.

Most of us require cars. We all understand their utility. Most of us have a sense of style, and we know beauty when it drives past us. And most of us have egos, and we know the thrill of acceleration when the pedal is under our right foot. So, when we combine these three things, we are left with no doubt that the sports car is a crown jewel, the flagship possession in our material portfolio. Desiring a sports car and being able to afford one are different things, and that's why they make *so much* sense.

WHAT'S IN A NAME?

When yielding to the desire for the ENGINE, the first thing to consider is, which car is right for us. As with any addition to any portfolio, its components must complement each other. They must work together.

ENGINE isn't just about speed. It's about f*cking up our entire life. The car that contributes most effectively to that goal is the right car for us

With that said, name brands are the way to go. These are big-ticket items (SPEND), high-octane jealousy stimulants (LEAVE), and the riskiest rides (WAGER.) Each step feeds the others. Mercedes, Jaguar, and Porsche satisfy not just the cost and ego components; their status burns[2] your social circle.

H O T   T I P

For maximum impact, the components of your
portfolio must complement each other.
Each step of my SLEEPWALK™
program must feed the others.

In a world of low-emission, low-carbon, low-class environmentalism, low "miles-per-gallon" is the new green:

---

2   Jealousy, competition, and bragging are all optimised. See chapter 2 for more f*cking stupid ideas.

ENVY

If we want people to think we are doing well — and we *do* — there is no sweeter cherry. Flashy and expensive to buy, run, and maintain, sports cars leave the rest behind.

Breathe my fumes, muthaf*cka.

Whatever financial position we are in before purchasing this beast, the process will cause a) acute pain at the front end and b) chronic pain thereafter. The cost of fixing, running, and insuring sports cars will leave us spiritually, financially, and emotionally running on empty.

And if the purchase is a stretch in the first place, and we think it wise to go the second-hand dealership route, this opens additional dead-ends. Cold dealers will take advantage of us via smooth sales pitches that paper over resale depreciation. We will pay too much and f*ck any hope of getting it back.

DETAILING

Then there's the upkeep: Change the tires — tune it up — only the best petrol, personal washes, and services will do. The devil is in the detailing. At £70 a clean, it's one more vampire latched onto one more financial artery, one more nail in the foreclosure sign hammered onto our soul.

For servicing, there's no option: The main dealer marks up parts and service to the extent that it is as scandalous as it is magnificent. That applies to the work that was needed as well as the work that was not. If things go tits-up, the asset is significant, and there are leasing agreements that can allow us to keep the wound open and the haemorrhage flowing.

IN CLOSING

My ENGINEs were a 3-litre XJ40 Jaguar gas guzzler, a Porsche Boxster, and a Mercedes-Benz SLK. Lovely and expensive drives that I didn't need.

I crashed and burned — repeatedly.

You are welcome.

STEP 4 — EDUCATE

COUNTERINTUITIVELY, STEP 4 IN MY SLEEPWALK™ 9-step program is to EDUCATE. Before you dismiss this as bullshit, hear me out.

We have been indoctrinated since childhood to think that education is empowering. We hear a never-ending mantra of "learn, study, better yourself" that promises the life of our dreams. What is *not* indoctrinated is expressing our dreams, finding peace with who we are and having a vision for our lives. So, we grow up brainwashed that education — qualifications — is not the means to the end but the end itself.

And who is it that touts this message?

- Schools, colleges, and other institutions of learning — businesses that see us as paying customers.

- Corporations — that promise career development to qualified applicants, abuse the f*ck out of us while marking up our services 1500%, and then burn us. (The way they still entice us with some version of a career opportunity is analogous to giving a child a lollipop before they stuff them in the back of their van. Do not confuse their offers with their consideration.)

- Governments — that need their country's GDP to out-sell in the global market so they can buy weapons that they will probably ask us to use to fight their wars.

I'm not saying that getting smart isn't smart; I'm saying that the education-at-any-cost mantra has created a well-informed cluster-f*ck. It will consume our soul unless we are hyper-vigilant. And who da f*ck got time for that?

FEATURES AND BENEFITS

So, in our brainwashed state, we SLEEPWALK™ through life seeking success through the academic version of SPEND. We build college debt. We buy courses. We subscribe. We gorge ourselves on the intellectual equivalent of fast food[3] about as useful to our life as an upset stomach.

And the result is multi-layered.

Firstly, there are the costs. From purely a consumer standpoint, there is little to add here that is not, in principle, covered extensively in SPEND. What is particularly tragic about EDUCATE that is worth hammering home is the nerve of those who sell us words. We can't even drive, live in, or wear useless information. We listen to it. Maybe we write it down if we are diligent. Perhaps we are forced to regurgitate it at some point. All so we can earn a piece of paper that certifies us as a sucker.

---

3 We cover gorging on actual FOOD in step 9 — KFC.

Student loans are your friends.
But don't use them for EDUCATE. SPEND
and WAGER can do more with the funds.

Secondly — and this is where it gets interesting — the certificates we earn set us apart as being overqualified for many employers. It's a bad cologne. Yet we must avoid the temptation of taking stock of the situation and continue to SLEEPWALK™.

Stay the course. Then stay an evening course, gathering sucker scout badges of higher education that pull us further and further from that which might centre us.

Thirdly, with no direct connection between what our heart is calling out for and what our qualifications can attract, we bounce from one unsatisfying job to the next. We seek the holy grail and remain clueless as to why the emotional payoff eludes us. When our C.V. looks like a fast food menu, we become less and less desirable.

And so, the spiral continues.

ATTITUDE

There is a danger that a vocation may start to please us. Be on guard for these feelings, for they may derail us from f*cking up our life. We have mentioned in previous steps that all steps must complement all others.

H O T T I P

> Create a genuinely inescapable web of
> self-sabotage. Nurture the ability to call upon
> any step to reinforce any other. It will make us
> unstoppable in our pursuit of the irredeemable.

In the event of unintended enjoyment at work, we can dig deep in our LEAVE repertoire and tell our employers to suck a fat one.

Be superior. Report superiors to HR. Cause friction. Anger them. We must treat our employers as if they are our enemy. We should study Sue's Son's *The Art of Self Destruction*, and use its wisdom against our employers, loved ones, and most importantly, ourselves.

SUE'S SON SAYS:

"If you are secure at all points,
you are lying to yourself.
If you have superior strength,
remind yourself you lack where it counts.
If you are temperamental, that's good.
Pretend to be weak,
so that girls think you are sensitive.
If you are taking your ease,
take more eases.
If your forces are united,
tell them you don't like their wives.
If sovereign and subject are in accord,
get angry at those who care.
Attack yourself where you are loved,
appear where you are not welcome."

~Sue's Son's *The Art of Self Destruction*

After all, how many of those f*ckers have as many certificates as we do? It's OK — we earned it, we learned it. Fall out with our employers. Ensure that they let us go, never hire us again, certainly don't refer us, and aid us in so many other ways in f*cking up our life.

IN CLOSING

The pursuit feeds the emptiness. And the emptiness feeds the pursuit. So long as you are pursuing the wrong things. Stay focused.

I have done all these things. I know what the f*ck I'm talking about. Learn from me.

Get smart. Educate yourself.

Step 5 — PLATES

Before I serve you PLATES, we should pause and review some things we have established over previous chapters.

Keeping a high-altitude perspective on the philosophies behind my SLEEPWALK™ 9-step program will help us understand that these steps are not distinct tracks. This is not an a-la-carte selection. While it is necessary at first to analyse and dissect the program to ingest its ideas, the experienced SLEEPWALKER will transition seamlessly between modes.

It's like learning to drive a car. At first, there is a lot to remember. Once the techniques are mastered and committed to muscle memory, the driver needs only to concern himself with the cliff he wants to drive off. The goal is to be able to SLEEPWALK™ in your sleep.

With that said, let's look at the different dimensions of being we have already brought to the f*ck-fest.

SPEND f*cks us financially — a material f*ck.

LEAVE f*cks us emotionally.

ENGINES may appear to be a material f*ck, but its power lies in social cluster-f*ckage.

EDUCATE develops intellectual asset f*ckage and degrades energy.

In PLATES, we will destroy our mental health. It is the mind-f*ck.

DESTABILISE

When we look at mainstream pursuits, a picture of stability quickly emerges. Steady jobs, steady income, healthy work-life balance, good spiritual-physical well-being. Blah blah blah. Stability is the enemy of the mind-f*ck.

SUE'S SON SAYS:

If your enemy is stable,
destabilise that muthaf*cka.
If your enemy is balanced,
unbalance that muthaf*cka,

Spinning too many PLATES is our power tool — our drildo — for mind-f*ckery. Why have one job when two will exhaust us mentally and compromise both positions? Why have a well-paid job when low-paid jobs are more stressful, and by their very nature, require us to have more than one? Why work with balanced individuals when controlling, insecure, or ideally, passive-aggressive personalities cause more upset. And if we can get employed by narcissists, so much the better.

Unbalanced, insecure, needy colleagues sow self-doubt and drive teams crazy. Be on those teams, high five them, associate with them. Find them and join them. Dealing with people we hate will cause chronic erosion of our sanity and self-esteem. High five!

Before we apply for work, we must at least seek negative staff reviews, even if we choose to ignore them for strategic reasons at this stage of the hunt.

Research interviewers and
seek negative feedback.

FIND YOUR TODD

If Todd sounds like an ass-hat, call Todd up. Impress Todd. Schedule a Zoom call with Todd. Present yourself as a desperately overworked PLATE-spinner that predator Todd will recognise as his next victim. Let Todd hire you for less money than you need. Let Todd require you for more time than you have. Allow Todd to yell and berate you. Allow Todd to fire you.

GO FOR BROKE

This degradation is a vital component of our skill set. It also has a secondary purpose. Compromising mental well-being can expose pre-existing — if dormant — mental disease; the "addiction" set. Addiction can be triggered if that seed is already in our make-up. And if so, tap it. If we think we have nothing to lose *now*, just wait!

Spinning requires intense focus on many moving and seemingly critical pieces. The goal is to stretch ourselves too thin to fulfil any task adequately — read: lose customers — and crush free time — read: poor physical health or even death.[4]

Overextended employment and finances are great PLATES, but the opportunities don't stop there. Overextending socially. Overpromising. Setting unreasonable expectations. Offering services you can't deliver. Long commutes. Limited time. These all contribute to PLATE tectonic stress that can snap at any time. Simultaneously, they establish golden let-down opportunities. Why be a business disappointment when you can be a personal or family one, too?[5]

By living in fear, we can motivate ourselves to create "safety pillars" — multiple jobs if shit gets real in some other job. Underpaid over-employment is a PLATE best practice.

DON'T DIE... YET

Finally: a word on getting help — counselling.

We have stated that death is for pussies. Counselling has the combined benefits of staving off the ultimate LEAVE event while maintaining pain and discomfort as chronic stressors. The SLEEPWALKER who doesn't go more than a week without having to face the shitstorm he has authored doesn't know

---

4   While it may seem like the holy grail of self-destruction, death is for pussies. Where can you go from death? Nowhere. The expert SLEEPWALKER dances with destruction without committing.

5   It may seem contradictory to the LEAVE ethos to commit to personal relationships that require effort on our part. However, think "net gain": If forming a low-value relationship can deliver high-value PLATE pay offs, then the P&L (profit & loss or plate & leave - take your pick) remains healthy. It's always about the bottom line — always.

dick. Regular reminders are grist for our mill. Plus, therapists are expensive.

IN CLOSING

I have done these things — all of them. I've taken on too much work and responsibility and repressed too much of myself spinning paper PLATES.

Because that's all they are: paper. If they fall, it won't matter.

But don't tell the SLEEPWALKER that. He's too busy to care.

Step 6 — WAGER

Tᴎᴇ ꙅıxᴛᴎ ᴏᴛᴇᴘ ıɴ ᴏᴜɴ journey to the bottom of our soul is WAGER — better known as gambling — and it's a game multiplier or amplifier.

Like leverage, a springboard, or staff, WAGER is to take our spending habit discussed in the first step and raise it by an order of magnitude. We are talking "exponential loss" here. By tapping loans, cashing paychecks, and maxing out overdrafts, the financing options are plenty.

HOW TO MANAGE SETBACKS

Sure, we will have a few "setbacks" when we win more than we SPEND, but these occasions are rare. Don't worry; the casinos have got our back and will always ensure that, in the long run, our deficit continues along the right trajectory.

We need to use those occasional income windfalls and channel them to our advantage. There will be plenty of opportunities to invest in our destruction in other ways. Or we can keep a regular gambling schedule, and eventually, the line will point back in the right direction. Plus, talking about wins and not about losses helps with propaganda.

DIVERSIFY

Specifically, several vectors are available to us: Arcades, betting shops, casinos, horses, and dogs are all tried-and-true money pits. And new online opportunities appear every day.

As with spending, diversifying our gambling options is the key to maintaining a "can lose" attitude. There is never a bad time to put bad money on a bad table. There is always a good time to put good money after bad.

H O T T I P

Just like spending, overdrafts, loans, and credit cards are all top-tier strategic tools for digging ourselves the deepest hole quickest. Especially if we can bust out the credit card for the Hail Mary "Go Big" bet.

Go Big plays are the highest cost, highest risk, highest reward events in the gambling sector. In SPEND, we mentioned that no single purchase will ever be our undoing. They are screw-ups, but not cluster-f*cks or royal f*ck-ups. On the other hand, Go Big events have the potential to wipe us off the map. Have you ever noticed that the windows in Las Vegas hotels don't open? There's a reason why.

DEATH BY A MILLION CUTS

Lingchi is an ancient form of Chinese torture roughly translated as "death by a thousand cuts". The idea is that many minor injuries are more terrible than a single, decapitating blow. If Go Big is a gun to the head, online gambling — especially via phone apps — is our *Lingchi*.

And while we are discussing phones, only the best, please, with plenty of data and service add-ons. We would not want to have our 24/7 gambling portal interrupted because of poor service. *Ling-k'ching.*

H O T   T I P

Online and phone app gambling portals are our 24/7 Lingchi service providers. Stay connected. Ling-k'ching.

The genius of the WAGER is not confined to its direct financial impact. Its psychological corrosiveness is every bit as damaging. Addiction in its chemical form is easier to understand from a dependency standpoint and works something like this:

1. We do something that makes us feel good.

2. We like it, so we do it again, but it has less effect this time as our body adjusts.

3. We "up" our participation to attain that same high to compensate for our body becoming less responsive.

4. Not only do subsequent gambling sessions require increasing amounts to achieve the same feeling, but withdrawal also becomes increasingly hellish.

And so, the spiral continues until our body can no longer live without the addiction that is killing it. Either way, we will die.

Gambling is the same, except it doesn't just f*ck with our chemicals; it f*cks with our mind.[6] It is one of the hardest addictions to break and can eventually control our thoughts and behaviours. And the gambling industry banks on this — literally. Just as losing makes us depressed, when we are anxious, we gamble. We must be prepared to lose everything.

IN CLOSING

Gambling is perhaps the most potent weapon in our portfolio of ruin. If we can risk £20 to win £30, we can risk £20k to win £30k. Remember to keep asking the question: how can I thoroughly screw up my life?

Gambling is a guaranteed way to improve our debt portfolio in the fastest time and leave us devastated — financially, emotionally, psychologically, and most likely, socially.

I was a pathological gambler who lost everything, bankrupting my businesses and my relationships. My life was in the gutter.

If we want to destroy our life, gamble.

If not, get help.[7]

---

6   Some believe that psychological addiction *does* affect the chemical composition in our brain. Understanding such information might put us on the road to recovery — the antithesis of this program. If you are interested in that, then SLEEPWALK™ is not right for you. Information on Gamblers Anonymous can be found in the resources chapter.
7   Read my book, *Inside the Mind of a Gambler.*

Step 7 — AWAKEN

BEFORE WE START, IT'S IMPORTANT to point out the semantic differences between common perceptions of the word "dream".

The dreams we live *for,* we will call *Aspirational Dreams—* AD's.

ADs give us purpose, meaning, and courage. They are the dreams people post about on social media in the hopes of being confused for some kind of guru of all things wise. "Follow your dreams." "Follow your heart." "Follow your passion." Horseshit like that.

The dreams we live *in,* we will call *delusional dreams* or double Ds.

Double Ds distract us, blind us, render us oblivious to all else. "Head in the clouds." "Living in a dream world." "Dream on, dude, it ain't gonna happen." "His head is so far up his arse; he can see out of his mouth." And so on.

In AWAKEN, awareness of these distinctions is essential.

Offensively, the goal of AWAKEN is to purge our *aspirational* dreams — to AWAKEN from their lure. We need to be conscious of them only to the extent that we can deny and repress them lest we inadvertently stumble upon joy.

Defensively, the objective is to protect the *delusional* idea that we are going about life in all the right ways. We must numb our aspirations and nurture our delusions. The SLEEP-WALKER must reject personal desires so that he can continue his mindless journey to nowhere.

DISCONNECT — DEVALUE — DISSECT

Those of us who are new to the SLEEPWALK™ program may still be aware of our aspirational dreams. It's important to have some connection with them by name, at least. Let's use marriage and kids as an example of an *aspirational dream*, well-documented as one of the deepest long-term sources of purpose, satisfaction, and joy. AWAKEN requires that we disconnect from that aspiration. One of the most effective techniques for bursting this kind of bubble is to pin fear onto it — to examine the worst-case scenario should the aspiration be realised.

Be systematic. List everything you ever wanted, and then dissect: What if we get divorced and I end up paying for lawyers and alimony? What if she is not who she appears to be? What if I turn out to be a failure? What if I can't provide?

H O T   T I P

> *The more we can associate our (previous)*
> *aspirations with terror, the less*
> *hold they will have on us.*

And notice that I have not said we must "kill" these dreams because we cannot kill our deepest desires. No. These desires are put there by a resilient universal intelligence far greater than we, to serve us as a guiding light and give our life meaning. No, sir. We cannot kill our innate passion, purpose, and want for love. We cannot snuff out the light we were gifted. We cannot mute our calling.

But we *can* repress the f*ck out of them and enter a spiritual and subconscious wrestling match that will never, ever, ever cease. Gagged on a conscious level, our inner voice will gnaw at our subconscious. Deep feelings of sadness, regret, and despair will course through us. And this will never stop if we keep holding on to those double Ds.

REMISSION

Aspirational dreams are like a cancer and must be treated as such. They never leave. At best, they go into remission. But be warned: there is never a time in your life when they cease to be available to you. We must chemo the f*ck out of them with toxic delusions and hope for the best.

But at any time, in a moment of weakness, love, meditation, despair, clarity, joy, humility, atonement, rebirth, analysis, or self-reflection, our true dreams and our true purpose can return. And stage-four purpose is a tough one to shake.

IN CLOSING

I have done all these things — all of them.

I have had to accept that not everything in life may manifest. I must be content with who I am now. I have learned that feeling angry and resentful about my past isn't going to improve my present or future. I have accepted this and learned to let go of deadwood.

Yes — stage-four purpose is a tough one to shake.

Step 8 — LOOK WITHIN

I CONSIDERED A FEW DIFFERENT titles for this chapter. "Shrinks and Repeat" was a contender, but I needed the "L" for my SLEEPWALK™ book. So, I went with irony instead.

LOOK WITHIN is sage advice in just about every self-help guide, spiritual practice, and religion. I cannot think of any form of healthy guidance that would suggest we don't. And while I believe that my 9-step plan is exceptional in many ways, it is not so exceptional that it does not include self-analysis.

But here is where the SLEEPWALKER is genuinely in touch: he knows that it's really f*cking hard to "go there", to open up and expose the raw emotions that real change requires we do.

DON'T TURN ON THE HEAT

Consider the garden variety "gym membership"; the membership alone does not build muscle. To affect real physical change, we must *use* the gear, put ourselves through pain, work, schedules, and recovery. If we do all that, then only after time might we see a difference.

Step 8 — LOOK WITHIN, is the equivalent of buying the membership but not doing the work. We can *say* we have invested in our growth. We can *say* we have committed time. F*ck it; we can even show people selfies from the wellness retreat that cost £3,500. What step 8 understands about human nature is that few people do the work.

So, what's the point? Why not just *buy* the membership?

Because we wouldn't be f*cking up our lives if we accepted that truth and were honest about that. There would be no wasted energy. No life force particles burned through for no good reason.

If we want to f*ck up our lives, we need to flirt with the "idea of growth" and convince our not-quite-subconscious that we are trying.[8] It's more painful and costly to be in a fake relationship with meaning. More corrosive to our self-image. More damaging.

Buy the eggs, whisk them, season them, and put them in the pan. But don't turn on the heat. This equates to all the effort, all the expense, all the time, and all the washing up. But no omeletto, Bro-ski. No omeletto.

START SMALL TO BUILD CONFIDENCE

Books are an excellent way for us to become familiar with the trap. Gurus will lure us with cheesy acronyms, easy-to-follow steps, and hot tips. They will tout reassurance that, if we follow their guidance, we too can do whatever the f*ck caught our attention that day.

Go for books that have cute little exercises at the end of each chapter that ask shit like:

---

8   There is, of course, no deceiving our actual subconscious. This imbalance leads to cognitive dissonance.

1. What did you learn from this chapter?

2. What will you do differently moving forward?

3. How have you gained wisdom from reading my horse-shit?

4. List ten people you feel you could impress by suggesting they could benefit from reading my books.

Writing shit down has the power to make us believe we are making progress. We think we are all scholarly because we had to get off our fat f*cking arse and find a pen and find some paper. And that's where the deception pays dividends. The guru de jour will blow smoke up our arse, promising us the change we wish for, and we believe it and yet won't turn up the heat.

And what happens when we don't turn up the heat?... no omeletto.

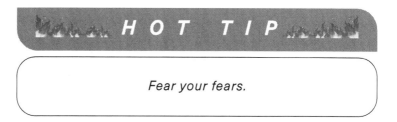

H O T   T I P

Fear your fears.

Books, therapists, retreats, spiritual practices — they are all the same. They will promise us the earth. Some may cost us the earth, too. They will ask that we face our fears to make "positive change".[9]

---

9   The single exception is my SLEEPWALK™ 9-step program. If you follow the steps, you will undoubtedly f*ck up your life. But if you don't, then you're just a f*ck-up. See? That's what makes my program different.

There is no greater source of paralysis than being so uncomfortable with whatever rejection we have a bug up our arse about that there is no way we are going to expose ourselves to that pain again. And when that happens, we begin to avoid trying new things. And that's when the fun starts.

EXPAND ON WHAT YOU KNOW

As with all the steps in this program, there are primary benefits and secondary ones. In this step, the secondary benefit is corrosion of self-esteem when not acting. It's more than simply not growing; it's hating ourselves for not even trying anymore.

Seminars are potent jabs. They are costly, they feel like a field trip, and we don't have to do much other than pay the fees and listen to wanker after wanker point to their shitty flip charts and power points. And for an additional £150 membership, they can f*ck us just a little harder.

Two weeks after this little adventure, and with no new "life opportunities" kicking down our door, self-reproach is our friend. Our friends are also our friends if we told them beforehand of our life-changing investment. If we call them up and ask them how they are, they will eventually ask us how the seminar went.

Perhaps we didn't change because we didn't sign up for the 10-day retreat. Fix that situation.

> When we f*ck up, double down.

Fill your calendar with a diverse portfolio of self-help foolishness. A solid plan will include an annual retreat, quarterly seminars requiring some travel and accommodation, therapy, and chronic reading.

IN CLOSING

I have done all these things — all of them.

I found that the idea of looking outside seeking guidance on how to look inside was an education in snake-oil salesmanship.

I was not looking *within*; I was looking with*out*, which left me *feeling* without.

STEP 9 — KFC

STEP 9 OF THE SLEEPWALK™ 9-step program — KFC — is the fast food health-f*ck. This step might seem lite compared to the industrial-strength cluster-f*ckage of, say, WAGER, PLATES, or SPEND. Nevertheless, it's the final piece in the holistic approach to a life well (and truly) f*cked.

Picture a scene in a film after a natural disaster mops up a family's possessions. They have nothing left. All gone. But then some smart-arse points out, "Well, at least we have our health."

Health is the thing that gives us reasons to carry on when all else is lost. Remove health from the buffet of little hope, and we cut gaping holes in the last safety net there is.

Conversely, if you fail at all previous steps but nail KFC, you are f*cked. Step 9 — KFC — kidney failure commitment — is the SLEEPWALKER's end game.

CONTEMPT

Step-1 of step 9 — and the only healthy thing about KFC — is to develop a healthy disregard for physical health in all its sneaky forms. Whether we nurture a mocking contempt towards gyms or hatred towards vegetables, these attitudes deter well-being. Blame it on the smell of sweat (in gyms if that wasn't clear) or the shitty music and lighting in Sainsbury's.

Derision of the routes to well-being — and those who take them — is critical to the upwardly-mobile downward spiraller. As soon as we convert the opinion that muscles-are-for-douchbags from conscious thought into a subconscious prejudice, the chances of working out drop like dumbbells.

With the goal of type II diabetes, heart disease, obesity, fatty liver, and clotted arteries, there are multiple routes to success.

WHAT'S ON THE MENU

Diet: The obvious starting place is fast food. High in fat, cholesterol, sugar, and convenience, and low in anything resembling a redeeming quality with the singular exception of cost, fast food is top in the menu of "death by..." options. It's the gateway drug to shitty health.

Exercise: Just don't. Take the escalator or the lift before you take the stairs. Take car services before you walk. Sit a LOT. Just don't exercise.

Sleep: When diet and exercise are under control (meaning out of control), we will be better positioned to rack up sleep hours, the critical metric for low physical vibrancy. Self-loathing grows without us even having to look in the mirror. Sleep is an excellent way to hide from reality. Lack of movement protects caloric reserves, and the wasted time contributes the PLATE tectonic stress.

Drink: Another fine avoidance substance. Beer is the SLEEP-WALKER's liquid carbohydrate of choice.

Chocolate: A subcategory that deserves special mention. Chocolate is an addictive overachiever that can fast-track progress.

When life gives you lemons, add sugar.
And when there are TV shows about
really fat people, watch them.

FAT F*CKS

Let's talk about fat f*cks. Belly fat is the "big dick" of high-achieving SLEEPWALKERs. The fat f*ck has done everything right. Note that there are two types of fat f*ck, he who tucks in, and he who does not. The fat *tuck* is a master of denial, while the loose-fitting t-shirt is a more mature traveller down the dead-end street of despair.

KFC can also lead to spectacular medical intervention, costly procedures to get the surgeon's knife, or lipo vacuum to do what your willpower couldn't. SPEND consequences to KFC strategies are great examples of outstanding step-networking. Remember, no step works alone.

Except, this step sometimes does.

FOR DESSERT

I have done most of these things. I have not done them all.

KFC is the step where your beloved author tripped and failed. I am still here. I needed to clean up my messes so that I could guide you through your journey. No other step will kill you. Some steps beg for relief, but KFC will turn the lights out. And ultimately, I fell short. And I believe that happened for a reason. If I can share the shame of failure, then perhaps you won't make the same mistakes.

For those SLEEPWALKERs hell-bent on destruction, I salute you and say only this: eat shit and die, muthaf*ckas. For the rest of us who fail to achieve total oblivion, we can at least convince ourselves that we gave it our half-arsed best. Some of us might even write a book dedicated to helping others avoid making the same mistakes we made.

How f*cked up is that?

In Closing

So, there you have it.

SLEEPWALK™ — Live in the Dream. My 9-step program of self-destruction.

Your demise is in your hands. I have provided you with a road map; it's your choice from here. After everything I have gone through, if you f*ck this up now, you really *do* need help, which is the point of this book: to be of help.

After everything I have gone through, if this doesn't make you feel better about yourself, one way or another, then I failed.

I hope that I have made you smile, even if it is at my own expense.

More importantly, if anything I said rang familiar, I hope my admissions — that no good came of this for me — are meaningful. If they contribute in any way to your search for happier paths, then this endeavour would have been worthwhile.

The following chapters are not a parody. They are the real me. I'll share where I am today and my road to recovery — from banning myself from betting shops to eating healthily to accepting the things I can't fix.

And I'll share specifics of the program I found invaluable in finding acceptance.

You may have noticed that SLEEPWALK™ always has that ™ after it. You likely assumed that ™ stands for "trademark". A fair assumption. I was deliberately misleading.

™ stands for total madness — the insanity of it all.

I've since changed it to SLEEPWALK®

®, of course, stands for recovery.

Step 10 — ACT

The great John McEnroe once said, "You cannot be serious."

To be clear, this book is a dark parody of self-help literature. The intention is to make fun of myself while talking about painful things. So, it's serious recovery presented in a ridiculous way. I hope you got some kind of kick out of it. So, as an opening up, this is the real me.

I have made mistakes, lived a dream that led to destruction, and expressed my competitive sportsman's instinct as a high-level tennis player. (I reached an ITF senior world ranking of 874). I always wanted to win. I hated losing. This competitive element led to competing with friends for materialistic success and refusing to lose. Ultimately, I lost many battles. I had to win when gambling! Win at all costs.

I was diagnosed with an anxiety disorder many years ago; it runs in the family. I've had dark moments. I've contemplated suicide as an escape from the pain life can bring. Unless you've been that low, you wouldn't understand. It's part of the human condition to experience suffering and pain. I aim to channel my life and experience positively to help others. I've trained as a psychologist and an acceptance and commitment therapist.

I've excelled academically — BSc (Hons) Psychology and MSc Sport and Exercise Psychology.

I've excelled in sport (reached my full potential).

I like working for myself.

I like writing books.

I have now reversed my health issues, stopped gambling, stopped competing with others and live a humble, accepted life. I am not trying to impress others. The cars have gone. I work for myself as a sports psychology consultant helping professional athletes going through the same struggles. I've realised now not to take life or people for granted. You don't know what you've lost until it's gone!

My brother is dead. My father is dead. I still play tennis for pleasure. I self-excluded from all betting shops. I had to stop. When you're told you have ten years to live, you have a choice — live or die. I lost over three stone, reversed fatty liver and pre-diabetes.

We are all just trying to survive in this life. I've cleared debts. I try to live without the pressures of society and don't buy expensive things I cannot afford.

I am now helping sportsmen and women to improve their mental skills; I understand what athletes go through in life and how events shape us.

So, to refute John McEnroe, I *can* be serious. And to wrap up this book, I will share how seriously I took my recovery and offer support to others who suffer.

WHY DO WE SUFFER?

Suffering is part of the human experience, which is the case regardless of material possessions and financial status. We can possess everything we could ever desire yet still feel depressed, unfulfilled, or even suicidal. We can appear on the surface to have everything — fame and success, an enviable life — yet be wholly lost on the inside, under deep psychological duress. Suicide rates are too high. Too often, we find ourselves in excruciating pain.

A fundamental characteristic of human life is psychological suffering, leading to anxiety, depression, and addiction. Mental health issues are rampant — a common contemporary malaise. As a culture, we struggle to manage life's demands. Sometimes, we look for relief in external material things: a sports car, a Rolex, nice clothes, a free lunch. Of course, these things are nice, but if we seek them to impress other people or mask our pain, it's a short-term, short-sighted strategy at best. It's an emotional band-aid.

I was like this for many years. Having attended many funerals in my life, including for close family members, I became increasingly aware of what people value in hindsight. No one talked about the watch of the deceased, the car they drove, or the money they had. Funeral conversations were more typically about fun times spent together; fond memories of experiences shared. As the saying goes, "you can't take it with you".

On reflection, I began to question what makes us happy — what makes *me* happy. Is it trying to get one over on someone else? There's always someone who has more than you — *upward comparison* — and always someone with less — *downward comparison*. It's a never-ending contest with no winners.

ACCEPTANCE AND COMMITMENT THERAPY

Many years ago, at one of his London lectures, I had the good fortune to meet the renowned psychologist, Dr Wayne Dyer. He teaches of finding peace, taming our ego, and living kindly. He teaches that "happiness is something that we bring to life", meaning: it's not something we can buy.

These were all lessons I needed to hear.

One of Dr Dyer's teachings that I found particularly resonant was about "letting go of false ideas", such as:

1. I am what I have.
2. I am what I achieve.
3. I am what people think of me.
4. I am separate from everything I want in my life.
5. I am separate from God.

This lesson is often challenging for us (me) to grasp. Our ego will object. When we link who we are with material items, success, and achievements, we move away from our natural source of identity. When the ego communicates "I am what people think of me", we attach *the self* and *self-worth* to material items. Don't buy into it. If we ever lose these material items, we lose the self-worth we attached to them.

Another lesson from Dr Dyer that I practice now is to stop fighting and controlling things — a classic source of stress and worry. We benefit from just letting things be. Dr Dyer talks about allowing the world to unfold, letting go of attached outcomes, allowing things to flow.

My interest in Dr Dyer's teachings started many years. Over time, I lost touch with his works. However, when I was training to become a psychologist, one therapy resurfaced. ACT — *acceptance and commitment therapy* — was developed by Dr Steven Hayes, who has since become a valued friend.

Sometimes in life, we may feel as if we live like we are sleep-walking, on autopilot and unaware of, or not looking, where we are headed. Then, one day, we crash and burn, which wakes us up. But by then, it may be too late to fix the damage we have caused. We may find ourselves in a deep hole.

After years of suffering debilitating panic attacks, I was hospitalised for a suspected heart attack. ACT taught me to stop fighting the panic and accept the feelings as normal. The ACT model of psychological flexibility offers an insight into the different psychological processes that help improve our experiences and live a more value-driven, fulfilling life. For example, a person suffering auditory hallucination is still a human being. The important thing is not the hallucination but rather the way they respond to it.

In ACT, metaphors are used to help those with psychological issues learn how to live a more fulfilled life and accept that pain and suffering are all part of the gig. For example, when I was at the height of my panic disorder, I couldn't even step foot on a tennis court (a life-long passion) and I had trouble queueing up (a life-long bore). It was a terrible experience. The feelings that came with it were debilitating. ACT helped me see that anxiety is normal and not something that I will ever get rid of. So, I needed to accept the feelings, stop fighting them, and engage in behaviours that moved me towards my values — towards a more fulfilled life overall. The alternative is to try and avoid anxiety at all costs. This isn't living.

As one of my teachers, Russ Harris, says, "don't feed your anxiety monster."

ACT: A MODEL OF PSYCHOLOGICAL FLEXIBILITY

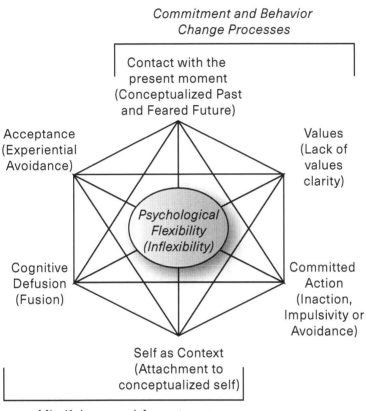

Commitment and Behavior Change Processes

Contact with the present moment (Conceptualized Past and Feared Future)

Acceptance (Experiential Avoidance)

Values (Lack of values clarity)

Psychological Flexibility (Inflexibility)

Cognitive Defusion (Fusion)

Committed Action (Inaction, Impulsivity or Avoidance)

Self as Context (Attachment to conceptualized self)

Mindfulness and Acceptance Processes

Copyright Steven C. Hayes. Used by permission.

ACCEPTANCE/EXPERIENTIAL AVOIDANCE

One part of ACT processes is *experiential avoidance*, which means: we will avoid unpleasant experiences, especially if they increase anxiety or things make us feel uncomfortable. For example, if we have anxiety about visiting shopping centres, we will avoid them, or if we have anxiety about queueing, we will avoid that. The alternative to *experiential avoidance* is *acceptance*.

To overcome this paralysis, we must learn to accept difficult thoughts, feelings, and sensations without letting them run and dictate our lives. We must learn to be comfortable being *un*comfortable. We won't ever get rid of anxiety, so we must find peace living with it.

We must accept psychological pain as part of being a human being. It's normal. We can learn from it: we can divert our attention towards choosing life-enhancing behaviours.

I have had to accept where I am in life. I can't force things to happen. I have learned to be grateful for where I am and what I have. I have found that making *upward comparisons* or competing against friends doesn't improve my life. On the contrary, it makes it worse. The message from ACT that transformed my outlook was to accept who we are and *where* we are, align our values, and make consistent behavioural choices that move us in that direction. And I remind myself daily to commit to this, stay in the present moment and have a flexible mindset.

COGNITIVE FUSION AND DEFUSION

Cognitive defusion/fusion is the idea that people can *"hook"* onto difficult thoughts and, similarly, let go or "unhook". When I "fused" with the thought I was having — *I'm going to die* — I tended to avoid the thought, to run off or escape (*experiential avoidance*). ACT helped me see that thoughts aren't literally true; they are just thoughts. We don't have to "hook" onto them. We can learn to observe them and let them pass. ACT has some great ways of dealing with thoughts and showing us how to observe them without "hooking" onto them.

1. Leaves on a stream
2. Clouds in the sky

Ironically, the more we try and suppress our feelings or thoughts, the more they increase — *ironic cognitive processes*, more commonly known as the white bear problem. (If I said to you, "don't think of a white bear for the next 30 seconds", you will no doubt have trouble doing this.) Similarly, it would be unproductive to suppress anxiety-producing material due to the *rebound effect*. The best thing I found was to allow the uncomfortable thoughts, feelings, and sensations to pass. I learned how to sit with them, observe them without letting them disable me.

I also used *cognitive defusion* or *"unhooking"* when I had thoughts about going to gamble. For example, if I thought, "I think my lucky numbers are coming in", I learned to let go of this and allow it to pass. Years ago, I would have fused or "hooked" onto this and then blown a fortune. Those of us with gambling problems may benefit from practising observing our thoughts without reacting to them. Remember, thoughts are just thoughts, and they aren't literally true! Allowing thoughts to pass through our minds is a valuable psychological skill.

It is all too easy to become entangled in a web of personal stories, worries, and diagnostic labels. I had to learn to see myself as a person experiencing panic, but I am not anxiety or panic. I am separate from this. These thoughts, feelings, and sensations do not define who I am.

It is also worth pointing out that our minds have evolved to be quite negative. They are genius at creating worst-case scenarios and tirelessly feed us. We have evolved this way so that our brains identify potential dangers — *fight or flight*.

It's hardwired. We can't rid ourselves of anxiety, but we can learn to live with it.

Consider anxiety an unwanted guest at a party. We shouldn't ruin our evening standing at the door waiting to stop them from coming in! That would spoil our fun. Let them wander around. Ignore them and focus on the guests we love.

VALUES

One of the core principles of ACT concerns living a value-driven and fulfilled life, as seen in the model of psychological flexibility. The value component is discovering what things are most important to us in life. It is too easy in the midst of daily life for us to lose sight of our "light house" or the direction we are heading. By rediscovering our values, we adopt behaviours that will move us in the right direction.

In ACT, there are two behaviour directions: 1. towards and 2. away from what's most important. The process we go through here is known as the "Matrix".

The matrix is a behavioural model that helps us identify a life problem, look at our thoughts, feelings, and sensations, and identify our current solution. Often, the current solution is a temporary fix. It results in "away" moves — behaviours that move us *away* from our values. The next step in the model is to identify what behaviours we could adopt that move us towards our values.

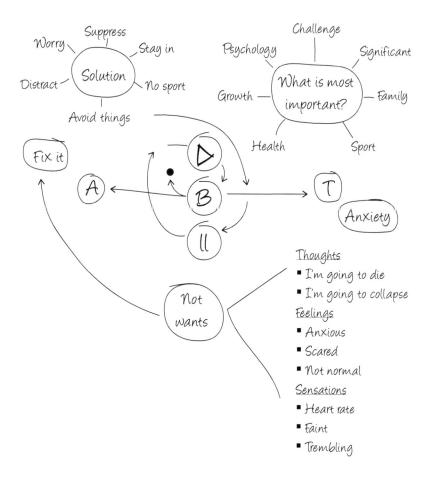

For example, if the issue is anxiety and our current solution is to withdraw, the result is an unfulfilled life. A *new* solution might be to go for a walk in the forest or meet a friend in the park. You take the uncomfortable feelings of anxiety with you while still doing behaviours that move you towards your values, ultimately resulting in living a more fulfilled life.

It took me two to three years to get back on the tennis court without feeling like I was going to collapse. This behaviour change was made from changing the current solution —

avoiding tennis due to anxiety — to the new solution — playing tennis but allowing the anxiety feelings to be there.

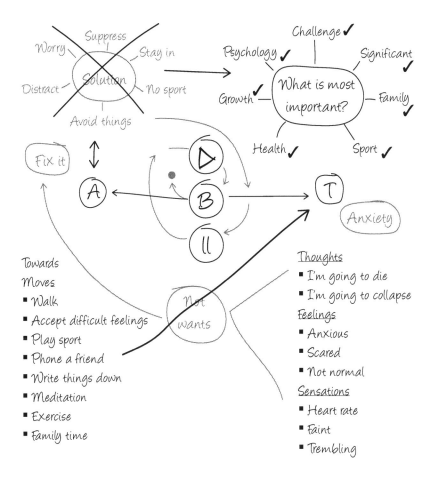

Identifying and addressing the solution was the catalyst for change. The worst thing to do is avoid a situation that causes anxiety. That won't fix the issue. We must learn that it is normal and learn to live with it.

Don't feed your anxiety monster.

SELF-AS-CONTEXT

My dog always appears to live in the present. I've never heard him complain about the past. What a way to be!

The present is all we have. However, due to our language and verbal functioning, we can disappear from the present moment. The mind is skilled at diverting our attention away from the present, focusing on past mistakes or creating future fears.

Self-as-context means *perspective-taking* and has commonly been referred to as the *conceptualised self*. If you have ever felt "in the zone", that's the same thing.

In ACT, the *self* can split: the *conceptualised self, self-as-on-going-awareness,* and *self-as-context*. In a nutshell: we need to be present and flexible when difficult things show up — being aware of our thoughts but realising that we are not our thoughts. One technique I find helpful in my recovery is the *"over-enthusiastic assistant"* — a thought process whose job is to pass on mind memos all day. This is a metaphor, of course.

We can observe the thoughts — memos —a nd choose how to file them: *read-and-engage-with* or *thanks-brain-for-that*.

If we say, "thanks brain for that message, 1 will put that over here", we acknowledge the message without suppressing or avoiding it. Remember, repressing a thought can lead to a rebound effect — the white bear problem. Read and file the memo.

1 have found this metaphor a great way to stop me from dwelling on thoughts.

We must remember that our minds generate thoughts in their thousands. Psychological flexibility is a valuable skill to develop. Creating a name for our over-enthusiastic assistant helps bring an element of fun to things and helps to loosen us up psychologically. My PA was called David Brent, a funny comedian-type character. This helped let difficult thoughts pass by without me "hooking" onto them and leading to "away from" behaviours.

COMMITTED ACTION

This is the part where we must commit to living our values. When 1 decided to quit gambling when 1 felt anxious or depressed, 1 re-directed and would go to the gym or play tennis. This is ultimately a "towards" value move and leads to having a more fulfilled life.

The rule of ACT is that if we slip up, re-commit (commit — slip — re-commit). There is also the choice point in ACT, which helped put me in charge of my choices. It allows us to stop, press pause, and think about what we are doing before acting.

I learned to ask the question, is this a *towards* or *away from* move?

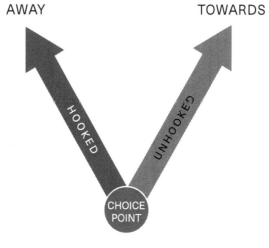

AWAY   TOWARDS

Situation(s)
Thoughts & Feelings

Choice Point 2.0 © Russ Harris, 2017 — adapted from the "Choice Point" by
Bailey Ciarrochi, Harris 2013

This is a simple tool. We live on autopilot most of the time, and by the time we wake up, it's too late. *Committed action* allows us to stop and think and then ACT. I had to learn to commit to making the "toward value" moves in life and stop living like I was hypnotised sleepwalking. If I was feeling depressed, rather than just sitting there wallowing in my negative thoughts, I would walk the dog, be in the moment with him, enjoy the fresh air. This is a "towards" move rather than an "away" move.

Remember that towards moves help us to live our values

and lead to a more fulfilled life.

CONTACT WITH THE PRESENT MOMENT

Years ago, I studied meditation, mainly to lower my blood pressure. However, with all the stress and time demands on my life, I forgot to keep doing it.

Sitting in a quiet place and having some "me reflection time" has many well-documented benefits to help calm the inner chatter. Even if I can meditate or just focus on breathing, it helps me reflect, plan, and make better choices for life.

I remember reading that we have 60-90,000 thoughts per day. Here's the depressing bit: most are the same as we had the previous day. My mind was filled with anxious thoughts, worst-case scenarios, and chatter. Once I took that time to "centre" myself (which ACT teaches), I was less stressed or anxious.

I also found peace in taking notice of things in the moment, e.g., the leaf on the tree, the feel of my coffee cup, or the words in a song I was listening to. Being in the present can help our psychological well-being.

I am now at the stage where I want to spend my days doing things I enjoy, e.g., sports psychology, lecturing, and writing books. I no longer feel the need to gamble, buy happiness, or compete negatively. I'm now giving happiness, helping other people with their struggles, and passing on words of wisdom so that others won't fall into the same traps.

I am AWAKE*.

RESOURCES

Acceptance and Commitment Therapy
Telephone: (03) 9015 9450
Email: admin@actmindfully.com.au
Address: Psychological Flexibility Pty Ltd
PO Box 31
Ringwood Vic3134

Acceptance and Commitment Therapy
Steven C. Hayes, Ph.D.
Foundation Professor
Department of Psychology /298
University of Nevada
Reno, NV 89557-0062

Gamblers Anonymous
The Wellness Centre,
45 Montrose Avenue, Intake,
Doncaster, DN2 6PL
info@gamblersanonymous.org.uk
0330 094 0322

Samaritans
Tel: 116 123
jo@samaritans.org

Sport Psychology Support

Hub 13A Pepper House

Pepper Road

Hazel Grove

Stockport

SK7 5DP

www.renwick.fitness

steve@renwick.fitness

SYNOPSIS

Straddling both sides of the foul-line — over-educated psychologist on one side and hyper-competitive, fear-driven obsessive on the other — Stephen Renwick is an eminently qualified therapist. He will not only guide you on how to screw up your life, but more importantly, he will show you *why*.

His latest gem — *SLEEPWALK™ — Live in the Dream* — provides a detailed roadmap to multi-faceted personal ruin via clear steps, real-world testimony, hot tips, and inspirational quotes. This tome leaves no stone unturned to leave no life unscathed.

Savage in approach, the author's mock 9-step program is a punchy, dark, and unrelentingly irreverent parody of the self-help genre. Yet, as hysterical as it is pseudo-smart, the humour is entirely at the writer's expense. At its heart, this is a confessional. That is what makes this assault so touching. Few could be so honest. Fewer could be so funny whilst being so honest.

Whether you are confronting your own demons and seek some perspective or are simply looking for an opportunity to laugh at the mistakes of another, or both, this book is a smart celebration of irony, wit, insight, and humility that will leave the reader feeling better for the experience. And you can trust Renwick on this; he's a psychologist.

Other books by the author:

 *Tennis is Mental*

 *Tennis is Mental Too*

 *Inside the Mind of a Gambler*

 Charlie and the cookies

Printed in Great Britain
by Amazon

81460322R00048